BABA YAGA

In the middle of the forest there was
a wooden hut that walked around
on chicken feet.

In the hut lived Baba Yaga,
the bony-legged woman.
Baba Yaga was so fierce that everyone
trembled at the sound of her name.
She had eyes like wet licorice
and skin like crumpled paper.
Her terrible teeth were made of iron
as strong as railroad tracks.
When Baba Yaga got into a rage,
she spat streams of fiery sparks.

3

Now, at the edge of the forest
there lived a little girl.
Although she was small,
she had a kind heart.

The little girl went into
the forest to pick berries
for her mother and father.

She did not know about
Baba Yaga, so she was
very surprised when
the bony-legged woman
jumped out from
behind a tree and grabbed her.

5

"What are you doing in my forest?"
screamed Baba Yaga, showering out hot sparks.

"I didn't know it was your forest,"
said the little girl. "I was gathering berries."

"My berries!" shrieked Baba Yaga.
"Mine! Mine! All mine! You must pay for them
by working here for three days!"

"All right," said the little girl.

Baba Yaga picked her up, tucked her under
a bony arm, and ran with her to the hut, which
was walking back and forth on its chicken feet.

7

"Day one!" screeched Baba Yaga.
"Clean my hut!"

"All right," said the little girl.

How dark that hut was!
How dismal with dirt!
No light could enter the windows
and no bare board could be seen
under all the dust and drippings
of old food.

The little girl set to work.
She swept and dusted
and scrubbed and polished
until the hut was as fresh as
a newly opened flower.

"Dear hut," said the little girl,
"you look very beautiful."

"Ah, little sister," said the hut
in a faint, shivery voice,
"you have a very kind heart."

The next morning,
Baba Yaga cackled,
"Day two! Cut me some wood
and stack it for my fire!"

"All right," said the little girl.

She went to the tall trees and
asked them for dead branches.
These she dragged back to
the hut. She cut them
and stacked them on
the newly cleaned hearth.

10

"Dear wood," she said,
"you smell of sunshine and rain."

"Ah, little sister," said the wood
in a dry, cracked voice,
"you have very kind hands."

11

The next day, Baba Yaga howled,
"Day three!
Polish my cooking pot!"

"All right," said the little girl.

She took the big cooking pot
and scraped off the soot
and grime. Then she rubbed it
with a cloth until the pot
glimmered like gold.

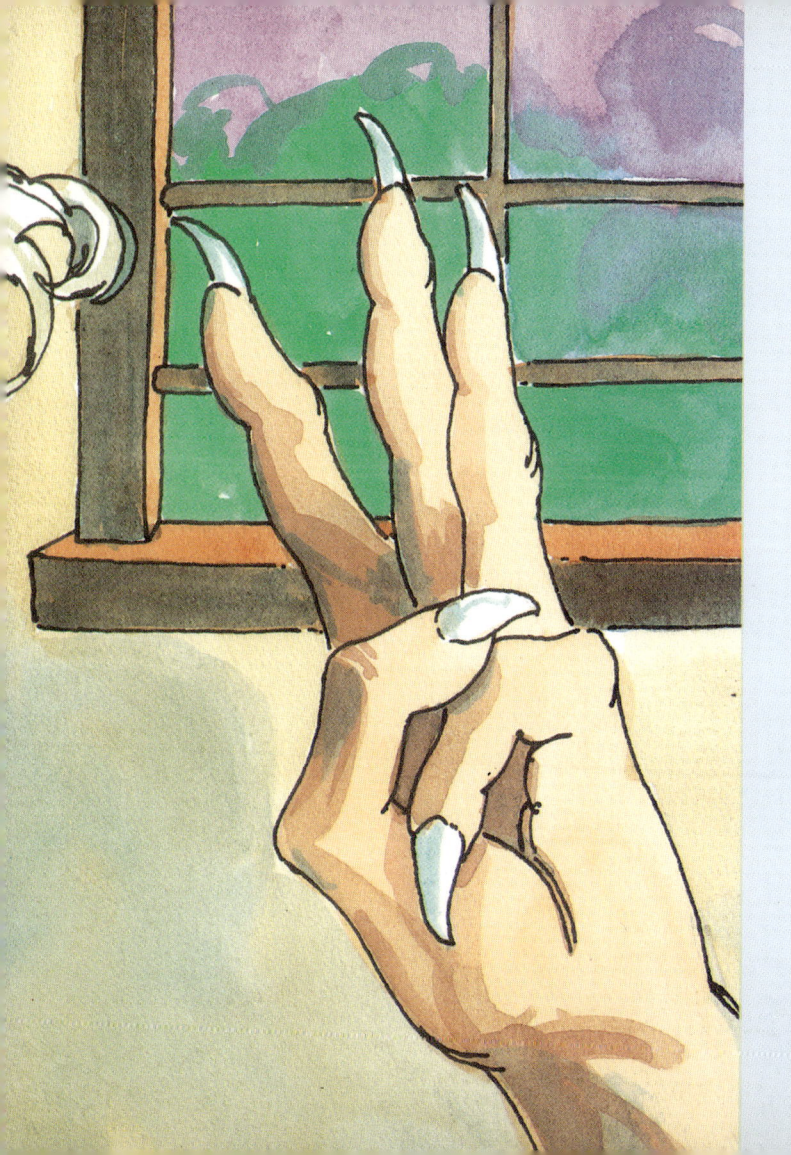

"Dear pot," said the little girl, "I can see my face in you."

"*Ah, little sister*," said the pot in a soft, shining voice, "*you have a very kind smile.*"

When Baba Yaga came in,
the little girl said,
"I have worked for three days.
Now, if you don't mind,
I'd like to go home
to my mother and father."

"Home?" yowled Baba Yaga.
She gave a horrible laugh that
showed all her iron teeth.
"So you'd like to go home!

Do you know what I'd like? Little girl stew with dumplings!"
Then Baba Yaga lit the fire.
She filled the big pot with water and set it on the flames.
"When the pot boils, in you go!" she bellowed at the little girl.

15

They waited and waited, but the water in the pot got no warmer than a purring cat.

"Boil! Boil!" roared Baba Yaga.

"*No!*" said the pot in a soft, shining voice. "*I will not boil!*"

17

In a ferocious rage,
Baba Yaga grabbed
the stack of wood
and threw it on the fire.

At once the flames died down
to birthday-candle size.

"Burn! Burn!"
bawled Baba Yaga.

"No!" said the wood
in a dry, cracked voice.
"I will not burn!"

18

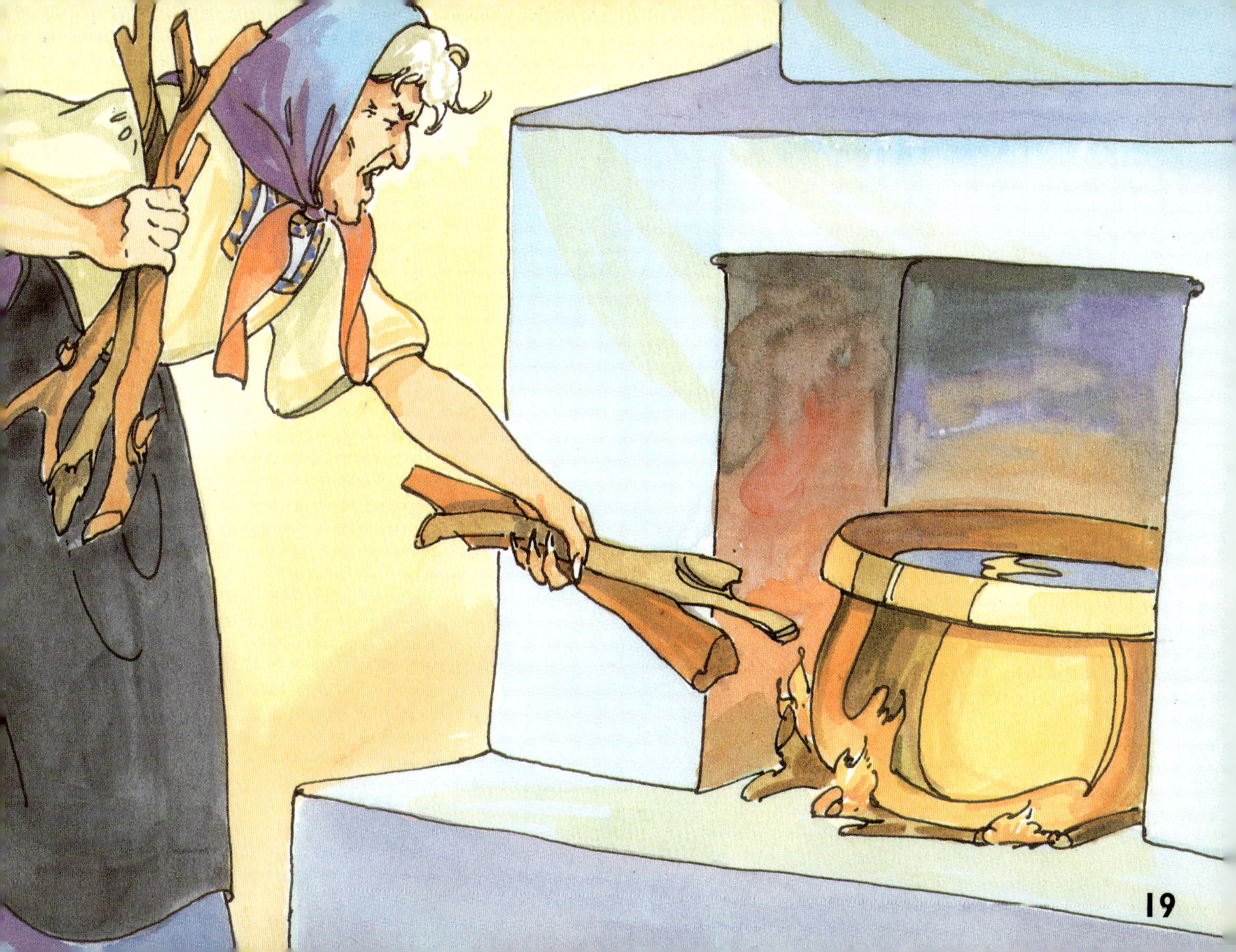

Baba Yaga gnashed her teeth
and sparks flew like hot, red rain.
She may well have boiled the pot
with her sizzling breath, but suddenly
the hut jumped up on its chicken feet.

The fierce woman lost her balance
and fell backward, her skirts over her head.

The door of the hut flew open.
"Run, little sister! Run!"
said the hut in a faint, shivery voice.

The little girl ran out the door
as fast as she could go.

21

Baba Yaga leaped up.
She would have caught the little girl,
but the door of the hut slammed
and locked itself on the outside.
Then the hut got up on its chicken feet
and ran away through the forest.

Baba Yaga screamed and raged,
sending streams of sparks up
through the chimney.
But every time she thumped on
the door, the hut went skippety-jump,
and she fell backward,
her bony legs waving in the air.

23

The little girl ran home, stopping a moment on the way to pick some ripe berries for her mother and father to make into a pie.

As for Baba Yaga, the bony-legged woman, she was never seen again in that forest.

Who knows where she might be now?